HOW TO BUY,
SELL AND RENT
IN NEW YORK CITY

For Dr. Dirk, my best friend and biggest supporter.

HOW TO BUY, SELL AND RENT IN NEW YORK CITY

The Insider's Scoop on Manhattan Apartments—
A Top Broker Tells All!

Heidi Berger

iUniverse, Inc.
Bloomington

HOW TO BUY, SELL AND RENT IN NEW YORK CITY
The Insider's Scoop on Manhattan Apartments—
A Top Broker Tells All!

iUniverse books may be ordered through booksellers or by contacting:

iUniverse
1663 Liberty Drive
Bloomington, IN 47403
www.iuniverse.com
1-800-Authors (1-800-288-4677)

ISBN: 978-1-4759-4455-6 (sc)
ISBN: 978-1-4759-4456-3 (ebk)

Printed in the United States of America

iUniverse rev. date: 11/14/2012

3-FREE OFFERS!!

1. Get a market evaluation of your property at **NO CHARGE.**
2. Ask me for help navigating the New York City real estate maze.
3. Receive my Quarterly Real Estate Newsletter. Send me your e-mail address and I will add you to my Quarterly mailings.

How to Reach me:

e-mail: heidiberger@mac.com

I look forward to hearing from you.

Best of luck with your NYC real estate experience.

Heidi Berger

THE INSIDER'S SCOOP

You are about to discover "inside" information from me, a top New York City Real Estate Broker so you will be totally prepared to successfully buy, sell or rent an apartment in Manhattan. I will tell you what the "experts" already know. These facts are current, up-to-date and comprehensive.

I am the "insider" with all the facts you need to know to make a successful real estate transaction. As a broker with over 20 years of experience I've seen it all. And I'm about to tell you how to do it right—and save you money, time and aggravation.

If you're thinking about getting involved in this market, you owe it to yourself to get all the information you need to make the smartest choice possible. This book contains all the facts necessary to guarantee that you will make the correct decision, given your special circumstances and your financial picture.

This is a subject that inspires huge emotional swings in people who are normally cool, calm and collected. It invokes anxiety and high stress. This book will give you the tools that allow you to gain control over the apartment situation by demystifying the entire process. It will give you key information that you need for a successful exploration of the market. You'll learn to be the one in charge—and you'll automatically feel better because you'll be the master of your own fate. Here are some of the important points covered:

- Discover the key to buying, selling or renting—learn the "Insider's Techniques" for getting the best deals.
- Learn about the Board of Directors in coops and condos and the power they have. Discover the secrets that will get you approved by the board.
- Unravel the secrets needed to understand the financials of a coop or condo. Learn about contingency clauses, mortgages and more!
- Find out the truth about giving a broker an exclusive—and how to make it work for you.
- Discover the differences between condominiums, cooperatives, rentals and sublets—and how to decide which one is right for you.
- Learn how to pick a real estate agent and the best way to get the most out of your relationship with them.

Chapter 2 explains the differences between coops, condos, rentals and sublets. Determine if you're a renter or buyer and discover what you'll need to earn in order to qualify for a rental. Find out what Board Approval is all about.

Chapter 3 tells you everything you need to know about the buying and selling process. This includes techniques for getting the best price for your property and more in-depth information regarding the Board Package and Board Meeting. You will learn what exclusives are all about. Discover the best way to market your apartment. Learn to read the financial statement of a building and discover how to fill out a board package. Also, find out the best way to get a mortgage.

Chapter 4 gives you descriptions of the neighborhoods where you can live.

You're now on the way to learning what it takes to close that deal, just the way the pros do it. By getting an "Insider's Look" at the real estate market through the eyes of an experienced and successful broker you'll gain confidence, assurance and savvy. It will take a lot of the worry and hassle out of your decision making process.

CHAPTER 2

Everything you Need to Know about Coops, Condos and Rentals

Apartments in New York City fall into several categories: condominiums, cooperatives, condops, townhouses, brownstones, lofts and rentals. They come in many shapes and sizes, including hi-rises and smaller buildings—with or without doormen. Architecturally they are either prewar or postwar construction.

The Differences Between Prewar and Postwar Apartments

Prewar means the apartments were built before World War 2. Typically they have beautiful crown moldings and high ceilings (at least 9'). Some have wood burning fireplaces, interesting archways and a lot of space. However, there can be some negatives. Sometimes they are dark and don't have any views. The bathrooms and kitchens tend to be older, some are in need of extensive renovations. Closet space can be challenging. Many of the buildings are given landmark status, making change difficult without bureaucratic hassles and legal fees. After all, who in their right mind wants to get involved with city agencies if it isn't absolutely necessary. And, like a rare fine wine, these precious apartments can be more expensive than the modern properties. There are many people who will do anything to live with high ceilings, moldings and fireplaces—all things that you don't get in the newer, more modern buildings, with cookie-cutter layouts.

Prewar doorman rentals are very difficult to come by, since most buildings of this type have converted to coops. There are only a handful of prewar rental buildings to choose from. If you're lucky you may be able to find a co-op sublet you can rent from an owner. But, if it's a long term rental you're after this is not the way to go. Most coop sublets are limited to 2-years and this can be problematic if you need a longer term lease.

Postwar construction is, by definition, modern and bland. Some people have objections to them because they are cookie cutter—all the same, and lack the uniqueness of the apartments with the prewar details and lovely architectural details. For the most part the ceiling height is only 8 feet. However, there are benefits. For one, they have newer kitchens and bathrooms. Second, many have views, therefore tend to be lighter and brighter than their prewar counterparts. Because there are more of them they are easier to find and may be less expensive.

There are actually two postwar categories. Buildings constructed from the 1950's through the late 1970's are larger than condos and rental buildings built beginning in the 1980's.

Charm vs. Pragmitism—The Choice is Yours

With a few exceptions, most brownstones, townhouses and lofts are prewar. People like them for their charm, spaciousness and uniqueness. They also tend to be smaller and more intimate buildings, providing an extra sense of privacy. However, there are some drawbacks. Lack of light is often a consideration. There may not be washers and dryers available to tenants. Sometimes the kitchens in brownstones are small and inadequate. The buildings were originally built as 1-or 2-family homes. When they were divided up into apartments, kitchens were an afterthought.

Many of them have no elevators, so if your apartment is on the 5th floor, I hope you're in excellent physical shape. To illustrate this point, **I found a beautiful 1-bedroom floor-thru in a well-kept brownstone on 66th St. and Madison Avenue for a nice young man in the film business. A floor-thru is an apartment that goes from the front of the building to the back. It was charming. About 1200 square feet, it had a terrace, wood burning fireplace, crown moldings and exposed brick walls. It was light, bright and very quiet. Even the bathroom and kitchen had recently been renovated. It had a lot going for it. It was in a prime location, but there were some serious drawbacks. There were no closets in the bedroom and no elevator. It was on the 4th floor and the nice young man in the film business admits that the walk-up can be especially grueling, especially when he's carrying** packages. He's currently having second thoughts about his decision to live in a walk-up.

My darkest real estate confession: Whenever anyone wants to see a walk-up I give them the keys and wait downstairs. I'm simply too exhausted to make the effort. What's really scary is how many apartments I've actually rented and sold utilizing this method. Well, so much for the power of my brilliant sales pitch.

Another negative to living in a brownstone, townhouse and some lofts is that there is no doorman to screen people, accept packages, and in some cases, no on-premises superintendent to fix things. **In my case, a live-in super is crucial, because my husband and I have no skill in fixing anything in our apartment. We need a super just to change a lightbulb.**

As far as a doorman is concerned, he is also crucial to our personal survival. My husband is a psychiatrist. We have many "unusual" people trying to see him at all hours. We depend on our doorman to screen these people and take messages so that we are not bothered. In addition, doormen are a fountain of information. Mine act as mother substitutes. They inform me when alternate side of the street parking has been suspended or if I'll need an umbrella. There's something comforting about knowing they're there and that they care (or at least pretend to be interested in my welfare).

Besides, if gossip is your life, as it is mine, you'll never have a better source concerning the sordid details of your neighbor's lives. Trust me—doormen know it all!!

Security can be a major concern in a non-doorman apartment. This sad story happened to a beautiful young model. **Her prior apartment, in a postwar doorman rental caught on fire, destroying all of her worldly possessions. She was starting again and wanted the allure and charm of a prewar. She ended up with an enchanting 1-bedroom, complete with a sunken living room and beamed ceilings. It was located in the heart of one of the best neighborhoods on the Upper Eastside—Park and 65th. It didn't have a doorman, but she wasn't concerned. I was concerned because she attracted people like a magnet. Her 6' stature, long blonde hair and jaunty walk caused people to notice her. It wasn't long before she was followed home by the bad guys. She opened up her front door and they forced their way in, beat her up and stole her pocketbook. As soon as she recovered she called me to help her find an anonymous building like the one she previously lived in, <u>with a doorman</u>.**

As in life, there are positive and negative aspects to everything. Determine what's important to your lifestyle—charm or ease of living. Do you get many deliveries, do you mind walking up stairs, are uncoordinated and can't fix things around the house? Is security a big issue to you? If your answers are yes you might feel more comfortable in a doorman building with an elevator, where there is somebody available to help you <u>literally 24-hours, 7-days a week</u>.

Space

This is an island, with a very limited amount of actual living space. Everything is scaled down to Lilliputian sizes. New Yorker's spend thousands on "closet doctors" designed to give us more room. Yet the apartments still overflow with our excess belongings and we rent storage spaces to compensate for our lack of room.

Furniture that looked so attractive in your suburban house looks ridiculous in our more miniature spaces. **I once took out a terribly fancy lady from Long Island (wearing stiletto heels complaining non-stop about her achy-breaky feet). She burst into tears when I showed her the apartment her husband wanted. She lived in a mansion and played cards everyday with her cronies. She sobbed uncontrollably that New York closets would never be adequate for her designer wardrobe. I secretly laughed because she was such a misery. But of course I wasn't laughing all the way to the bank with that hefty commission. She won the war with her husband and they stayed where they were.**

Living here requires a certain mindset. There's never enough space, and yet we pay an enormous amount of money for the privilege of a New York City zipcode. After all, where else can you walk out your door and feel truly alive and exuberant. The seductress named New York City has cast her magic spell over us. We are hooked, addicted and envied by people all over the world because we live in the fabulous New York City.

Layouts

Learning the different configurations of space can be more confusing than studying a foreign language. That's why I am now going to give you definitions of terms and average square footage you can expect.

The smallest layout is the **"straight studio"** (2-rooms) with about 475 square feet and the **"alcove studio"** (2.5-rooms) with approximately 550 sq. ft. The alcove studio is sometimes referred to as a Junior-2. This means there is the ability to put up a wall in the alcove to make it a very small one-bedroom.

The straight **"one-bedroom"** (3-rooms) is the next size up. They range from 600-700 sq. ft. After that is the **"Junior-4"** (3.5 rooms). This is a one-bedroom with a separate dining area. Some people in need of two-bedrooms convert the dining area (usually a dining-L) into another room. You can put up a wall (with permission of management) or screen. Sometimes they have a bath and a half, or 2-baths. These apartments can range anywhere from 750-1100 sq. ft.

A straight **"2-bedroom 2-bath"** (4-rooms) is next on the list. A two-bedroom with <u>split</u> bedrooms is one in which the bedrooms are on either side of the living room. Most people prefer this layout instead of a 2-bedroom with the bedrooms right next to each other. They range between 950-1100 square feet.

Next up is **"2-bedroom and dining area"** (4.5-rooms).** This is a 2-bedroom and a dining area or den. New Yorkers' always hungry (desperate) for more bedrooms sometimes convert the dining area into another bedroom. They range between 1200-1600 sq. ft.

A very common and popular prewar layout is called a **Classic Six"**. People like these layouts because they tend to be spacious and have more charm than their postwar counterparts. They consist of 2-bedrooms, 2-baths, a maid's room with a small bathroom, formal dining room, entry foyer, kitchen, and in some cases a pantry. The square footage is in the 1400-2000 range.

The prewar "**Classic 7 is 3-bedrooms 3-baths"**. It has a maid's room with a small bathroom and a formal dining room. Most also have an entry gallery and kitchen with a pantry. Square footage is in the 1800-2500 range.

There are larger apartments, some with 14-rooms found on Park and 5th Avenue. If you really want privacy and space, a townhouse is the way to go. Obviously these are much more costly options.

Renovations

Once in a while there is the possibility of combining apartments either next door or upstairs and downstairs to create a duplex. You need to be lucky enough to find these opportunities and then you need money. Or maybe you just want to update your bathrooms and kitchens. Whatever the case if you're renovating you'll need the services of an architect to get you through the process. There are many forms to file with the city in order to get the necessary permits to do certain types of construction, such as combining apartments. You also have to get everything approved by the Board of Directors of your building as well as your management company. This includes submitting architects plans and a renovation agreement. Things take a very long time not only to get approved but to get done. So, make sure your schedule is flexible. Also, all buildings have different rules. Some only let you work in the summer, and others limit the amount of time you have to get the work done otherwise big fines start to accrue. In my building, for example, work can commence at 10AM and must end at 4:00PM weekdays only.

Make sure your contractor has the necessary insurance and certifications to do the job. Also, buildings require owners to sign building alterations agreements. This is an agreement between the building and the owner, in which the owner agrees, among other things, to submit plans to the board of directors for approval, provide necessary insurance and make sure that the contractor does not file a mechanics lien against the property. Once this is signed and the plans have been approved, the plans cannot be changed again without further board approval. **I just lived through a gut renovation of my place—it is not for the feint of heart. I ate sedatives throughout the entire process.**

Not all buildings allow washers and dryers in the apartment. In some cases you'll need permission from management, which is not always readily available. In a rental building chances are not good. **I just lost a $3 million dollar deal because of a washer dryer debacle. The broker told us it was allowed in the apartment and the contract was signed. Right before we closed, the buyer discovered he could not have a washer dryer. Now there is litigation as the buyer tries to get his $300,000 contract deposit back because he was deceived. It is a cautionary** tale—make sure before you sign a contract that you hire a lawyer who will do due diligence on the building to find out what the rules and regulations are.

Co-Operative Buildings

According to Douglas Elliman, coops are not a new concept, although they seem to be a type of ownership mostly in New York City than elsewhere in The United States. In New York City, approximately 80% of apartments available for purchase are in cooperative buildings, while 20% are in condominiums. This means two very simple things to potential buyers in New York City:

1. There is more inventory to choose from if the buyer includes co-ops into the mix and,
2. Prices are, in general, more attractive for cooperatives.

Cooperatives are owned by an apartment corporation. Individual tenants do not actually own apartments as they would in the case of "real" property. Owners (shareholders) of co-op apartments actually own "shares" in the corporation which entitles them to a long-term "proprietary lease". The corporation pays the total amount of the building's mortgage (importantly, a co-op may have an underlying mortgage on the entire building, whereas a condominium building must be owned outright). The monthly maintenance in a coop goes towards real estate taxes, employee salaries, and other expenses for the upkeep of the building. The tenant-shareholder, in turn, pays a portion of these expenses as determined by the number of shares the tenant owns in the corporation. Share amounts are dictated by apartment size and floor level.

The considerations when buying a cooperative are:

1. The Board of Directors has the right to "approve" or "reject" any potential owner. The Board, elected by all of the tenant-shareholders of the co-op interviews all prospective buyers. It has the responsibility of protecting the interests of all tenant-owners by selecting well-qualified candidates.

2. The quality of services and the security of the building are kept at high standards.

3. Portions of the monthly maintenance are tax deductible. Each building has its own tax structure but all co-ops offer a tax advantage. Shareholders can deduct their portion of the building's real estate taxes, as well as their proportionate share of the interest on the building's mortgage.

4. The amount of money that may be financed is determined by each cooperative. Some buildings require substantial down payments. Generally speaking, in Manhattan, prospective purchasers should be prepared to "put down" at least 20 to 50% of the purchase price (depending on the building) when purchasing a cooperative apartment. In addition, coops require that you must have **liquid assets** remaining after closing. Each building has their own formula for whether

the remainder of your financial portfolio, after the deposit is substantial enough to be able to pay the maintenance and live in the building.

5. Subleasing a co-op must be approved by the Board of Directors of the cooperative. Each corporation has its own rules, and they should be examined if an owner intends to sublet. Usually it is a 2-year maximum term, and permission for year two is given after year 1.

6. Co-ops sometimes charge shareholders a flip tax when they sell their apartment. This fee, which is usually between two and four-percent of the sales price, is often the responsibility of the owner.

7. If you are buying an apartment to use as a pied-a-terre check to be sure the building allows this scenario.

With this in mind, it is important to remember that co-ops are the norm here in Manhattan, not the exception. However, before beginning a search for a cooperative apartment think about the financing limitations and the sometimes grueling Board Approval process. You must divulge to the Board all of your very personal financial information in the form of the Board Package.

Condominium Buildings

While condominiums are quite common throughout the country, they are a rather new concept for New York City. A condominium apartment in Manhattan is real property. The buyer gets a deed just as if he were buying a house. Since this is real property, there is a separate tax lot for each apartment. This means the buyer pays his own real estate taxes for the property. An owner will also pay common charges on a monthly basis. Common charges are similar to maintenance in a cooperative. However, they will not include real estate taxes since these are paid separately, nor will they include the building's mortgage and interest given that a condominium, by law, cannot have an underlying mortgage. Condominiums are attractive for a variety of reasons:

1. Financing the purchase of a condominium apartment is governed by the financial markets' not a board of directors and thereby much more flexible than in a cooperative. Generally a buyer can finance up to 80% of the purchase price.

2. An approval process is usually required, and some condo boards require application packages with financial disclosure. Generally, however, the requirements are not as rigorous as the co-op boards. A board meeting is usually not required. The length of time for approval varies from building to building, but it is usually not as long as a co-op approval process.

3. There is greater flexibility in sub-leasing your apartment. This makes condominiums the better choice for investment property. However, check on the rules. Some buildings require a buyer to live there for a year or two, before subletting is allowed.

4. They are the ideal choice for non-U.S. citizens or for those with their assets outside of the United States given that co-ops are unlikely to approve a buyer whose funds are not in the U.S.

5. Closing costs for the condominium mortgage are higher than a co-op. The title search, which confirms that the owner has a right to sell the property and there are no liens against it is expensive. But a condo doesn't scrutinize your assets they way they do in a coop. This is why they've gained such popularity in the city.

6. Given that there are fewer condominiums than cooperatives, they are real property and are "easier" to purchase, they are generally more expensive than co-ops. Additionally monthly combined common charges and real estate taxes in a condo are typically less than a co-ops monthly maintenance charges, again resulting in higher purchase prices.

Steps to Purchasing an Apartment

The steps to purchasing a co-op or a condominium in Manhattan are very similar. Let us assume you have found the property on which you wish to place an offer and that you have spoken to a bank or mortgage broker (if financing) to determine a comfortable financing price level.

1. Offers are made orally in New York City. When you have found the right property, a bid or offer will be placed through your agent. They will

convey your offer to either the seller's agent or to the seller directly.

2. The seller may "counter" your offer. This will begin a negotiation process that will hopefully lead to a "meeting of the minds", at which point price, terms and closing date have been agreed upon.

3. A real estate attorney is required in all property transactions in New York City. Contact an attorney familiar with real estate in Manhattan to represent you. The seller's attorney will begin preparation of a contract of sale, and during that time your attorney will examine the financial condition, and do the general due diligence of the building in which you wish to purchase. Your real estate broker can assist you in finding experienced attorneys.

4. After your lawyer concludes that the financial condition of the building is satisfactory, that the by-laws of the building are acceptable to you, and that the contract of sales is also acceptable, your attorney will allow you to sign the contract. At that time you will usually be required to present a deposit of 10% of the purchase price. The contract plus the deposit will then be forwarded to the seller for signature. This money will be held in the seller's attorney's escrow account until closing. It is important to note that until all parties have signed the contract, and it has been delivered back to your lawyer, the seller can still entertain and accept other offers.

5. If financing, you should move forward with your loan application. Your real estate agent can assist

you in finding a mortgage broker. You should definitely get pre-qualified for financing with a mortgage brokerage firm prior to beginning your housing search.

6. You will, by now, have received from your real estate agent the board requirements and application materials. The application materials can be similar for a cooperative and condominium. However, the actual process is quite different. You will need to complete all the required materials which typically include: an application, a financial statement, all requisite support and backup for your financial statement, at least two years of tax returns, bank statements, letters of personal and financial reference, letters of professional reference, the contract of sale, bank documents (if financing) indicating that your loan is in place.

7. When your "package" is finished, your broker will review it, make changes and or improvements. This tweaking of your paperwork explaining your qualifications is probably the most important aspect of this process. The broker must make sure you are presented to the board in the best possible light. When it is satisfactory they will forward it to the managing agent for review. Upon determination that it is order and that credit checks were acceptable, it will be forwarded to the Board of Directors. No applications will be accepted by a Managing Agent unless they are complete.

8. In the case of a cooperative, if your application meets initial approval, you will be invited to be

interviewed by the Board or by an interviewing committee. This is a serious matter and not to be taken lightly. It should be treated as a business meeting. Dress conservatively and keep the conversation low key and as polite as possible. Remember this important point: Nobody has ever been rejected for being boring.

9. After approval by the Board, you are ready to begin planning for a closing! In the case of a condominium, there is generally no formal interview. Your application will be reviewed and if all required materials are included and in order, an approval is typically granted. The entire process can move quickly in a condominium, and assuming a loan can be secured in a timely fashion, one can move from contract to closing in about 60-days. However the cooperative process is more involved, and 60 to 90 plus days is not unusual.

Renting

According to Douglas Elliman, as a guideline, you can expect to pay 25% of your gross annual salary for rent. To qualify for tenancy, most landlords require that you annually earn 40 to 50 times the amount of the monthly rent. Remember to take into consideration outstanding loans and liquid assets. Major landlords are rigid in New York City and cooperative sublets can even be more demanding. You might find more flexibility with an individual owner in a condominium who wants to rent out their unit.

Lease Guarantors: If your salary level and total financial picture does not meet the landlord's requirements you will need a co-signor, or guarantor, to guarantee the lease. Landlords prefer a family member who owns property in New York, New Jersey or Connecticut. The guarantor must earn ample income, around 100 times the cost of the rental. Extensive financial documentation may be required and paperwork cumbersome. Employers will seldom guarantee on behalf of the employee.

Internationals: If you pay taxes outside of the United States, or if you have a housing allowance from your employer, your eligibility is evaluated differently. Your company's relocation department will be able to assist you with this.

Subletting Your Apartment

In a rental building, if the apartment is being sublet furnished, the tenant can charge an additional 10-percent over the current rent. If you are caught violating this rule the penalty can be stiff. In addition to the overcharge refund, the prime tenant may be required to pay the subtenant up to three times the overcharge. The original tenant must be able to prove they are returning at the end of the sublet. The law also states that a rent-stabilized apartment may only be sublet two years out of a four year period.

Step-By-Step Process to Renting an Apartment in New York City

1. Find a broker. This can be done by going to The New York Times Website (nytimes.com), and doing a search in the real estate section.
2. Organize the following information:
    *   Letter of employment and salary verification (include start date if not yet employed)
    *   Bank account numbers (checking and savings), credit card numbers
    *   Names, addresses and phone numbers of previous landlords
    *   Names, addresses and phone numbers of accountant and attorney, if applicable
    *   Names, addresses and phone numbers of personal and business references
    *   Tax Returns
    *   Pay Stubs
    *   Expected bonus (verification from employer)
    *   Additional sources of income with verification
    *   Driver's License or passport
3. If relocating, prepare the necessary funds before coming to New York. Landlords will not accept personal or out-of-state checks. They require certified funds.
    *   Try to establish a New York bank account before you begin your search. If this isn't

possible, bring the necessary funds with you.

- The broker's fee is 15-percent of the yearly rent. It is due upon signing of the lease, unless your employer is paying the real estate broker fee. You'll also have to pay the first month's rent and a month's security deposit.
- There will be a Credit Check done. This is usually $50 to $100 which can be paid by personal check.
- If you sublet a Condo or Coop there will be move-in/move-out and application fees which can be expensive. You won't have these expenses in a rental building.

4. The day of your appointment you will meet with your agent and be taken to the properties your agent has scheduled for you to see.

5. When you have made your apartment selection, you will be asked to fill out an application and other miscellaneous documents. If possible your agent will negotiate price and lease terms. Upon acceptance, a credit report will be done and your references will be checked.

6. Leases will be signed and checks presented to the landlord. If you have sublet a Condo or a coop you must fill out more extensive paperwork. With a coop you'll have to meet with the Board of Directors in order to be accepted into the building. There is usually a maximum of a 2-year term limit to a sublet lease.

Apartment Shares

If you can't afford to rent an apartment yourself, or want to live with a friend, there are a few rental buildings that allow shares. Under New York State and City regulations in a rental building, a tenant is allowed to share his/her apartment with one other person and that person's dependent children. Also, an owner or tenant (in a rent-regulated apartment) must reside in the apartment to have a roommate.

Because of the high cost of apartments, many people living in New York take on roommates. There are companies that specialize in finding roommates. You can Google the subject and get a list of companies.

I used one of these services when I first moved in to town too long ago to mention. I had just broken up with "the boyfriend from hell." It was an eight-year relationship that had been going downhill for seven-years. The roommate service was great because I was in a hurry, had no furniture and really needed to get settled with the minimum of hassle.

Everything was fine, except for my new roommate Susan. She had a "toilet paper fetish." She'd spend hours in the bathroom, using the toilet paper to wash and re-wash her face and hands. She'd spend hours trying on new looks with gobs of make-up. It was on-again and off-again for her eyebrows, lipstick and eyeliner. Sometimes she'd use up an entire roll in a night. And it was always everywhere, all over the apartment. There so much everywhere, and I was always getting tangled up in all of it.

I'll never forget the night I came home and found her hysterical crying. She had recently met a cabdriver on her morning ride to work. They quickly became engaged and he brought her home to meet his mother. She was sobbing because her mother-in-law to be accused her of using an excessive amount of toilet paper and she was too insulted for words. She just couldn't understand what she did to alienate her new "mom." Needless to say I was speechless.

The last straw was when a date I was trying hard to impress picked some of the toilet paper out of my hair. The next day I decided that I should live alone.

There are companies that put up walls to create an additional room. This is a good way to make a two-bedroom out of a one-bedroom. These pressurized room dividers look permanent but can be easily removed at a moments notice. However, some buildings don't allow them, so check before you do anything.

PETS

Verify that the landlord allows pets, prior to signing the lease. Many landlords that do allow dogs require them to be under 20-pounds. Some buildings actually require a meeting with the dog to analyze their potential for noise and trouble. Many condominiums have adopted strict no pet policies. Some allow owners to have pets, but not renters. Do your homework!

Condominium and Co-Operative Sublets

The beauty of a rental lease is that you can keep the same apartment year after year. As long as you pay the rent you can keep the apartment for years to come. If you know that your stay in New York will be limited, a condominium or co-op sublet could be the right choice for you. Most owners of these types of units will give you a one or two year lease.

In the majority of condominiums there are no rules about how long a condo owner can rent out his apartment, it depends what his individual needs and goals are concerning the length of lease he will give you. He may want to continue renting it out year after year. Perhaps at some point he will want to sell it, or move into it himself. If you can roll with the flexibility, this could work for you.

Condos have a board approval process called "the right of first refusal." Generally you'll have to fill out a board package with personal and financial information and have a credit check done. But in most cases you won't have to meet a board. Approval can take up to three weeks but if your paperwork is in order there shouldn't be a problem.

Strict co-op rules make these apartments more difficult to rent than condos. The Board of Directors dictates all the policies of the building so they tell the owners how long they can rent out the apartment and can accept or reject the potential candidate. Generally the sublet period is not longer than two-years. If you decide to go this route make sure you have plenty of time to wait for the approval. You've got to fill out the

Board Package and this paperwork tends to be very detailed regarding your personal finances. Approval requires meeting the board members and can take a minimum of one-month. If you're an owner thinking of subletting, call your building manager and find out what the rules and requirements are <u>before</u> you put it up for sublet.

To move in to a condo or co-op you'll need to give the owner a minimum of the first months' rent and a months' security. But if you have a pet or the apartment is furnished you may be required to put up additional security. If your landlord is an individual owner of a unit he is not required to pay you interest on the money. But, if he puts the money in an interest bearing account he is required to pay you, less a one-percent management fee.

Generally the landlord will want to add a renewal clause asking to be notified 60-days prior to the end of your lease concerning your intentions to continue renting the apartment. Also common is a show clause, which allows the owner to show the apartment at least 30-days before the end of your lease. You should be given 24-hours notice, with reasonable times and at your convenience.

If the apartment needs to be painted, or the landlord has agreed to specific repairs, this should be stipulated in the lease. Be sure that any agreed to increases or other details be put in writing as part of your lease. In addition, sometimes landlords add a penalty clause if the rent is not paid on time.

Before you sign the lease, ask the owner to give you the building's By-Laws or Proprietary Lease to find out about the buildings' rules.

Don't make any alterations without getting permission in writing from your landlord. If there is any minor problem when you're living in the apartment call the superintendent. If there is something major that has gone wrong, such as a faulty appliance call your landlord. In addition, both you and the landlord should have Homeowner's Insurance.

Be certain that you have a good relationship with the landlord <u>before you sign the lease.</u> Here's an example of a deal gone bad from Day One. **I rented a world famous European director a \$30,000 a month duplex with Central Park views in one of the most exclusive condos on 5th Avenue. It hadn't been easy finding him a place to match his requirements but finally, after many near misses I found him a glamorous apartment that spelled SHOW BIZ.**

It had every luxury imaginable, from the finest imported Italian marble, fabulous views and a sound system as sophisticated as you would find in any professional recording studio. It seemed almost too good to be true. There was something about the apartment that I instinctively felt suspicious about. Maybe it was the sleazoid broker who was in charge of renting and managing the apartment that made me uncomfortable. She was a pudgy big-mouthed monster with a hideous reputation in the small world of New York real estate.

Just before the owner countersigned signed the lease, I found the director the perfect townhouse just off Park Avenue. I begged him to take it. He said that he appreciated my opinion but he wanted his family to have "The New York Experience"

and felt that this fabulous duplex would allow him to live out his fantasies of living and working in the city.

He was due to move in at noon the following day. I was sitting at my desk with a thousand real estate nightmares on my mind when my phone rang. "Heidi" the unmistakable Shakespearean voice of the famous director dramatically said. "My wife and baby are stuck in the elevator in between the floors of the apartment." (the dump had its' own elevator). I panicked and raced right over. When I arrived, the wife and baby were just being extracted from the elevator by building security. I decided it was time for an in-depth inspection of their new home. To my horror I discovered the place was like a movie set. It looked great, but it was as if the place was built out of cardboard. Nothing worked. Not the fabulous sound system, not the beautiful Italian marble sauna. The drapes couldn't even be closed—they were on some sort of hydraulic system that seemed to be permanently stuck.

I decided to confront the monster broker immediately. Since she lived right in the building she came right up. She assured me these problems were only temporary and would make sure everything was fixed within a few days. The director and I decided to give her a chance to rectify the situation—although we both agreed our chances for success were minimal.

The next day the director's lovely wife, barely recovered from the elevator debacle decided to invite some close friends over for a traditional

English meal. She spent the morning planning the menu and buying the ingredients. As soon as she began cooking, the very proper English nanny buzzed from the downstairs intercom to tell her the baby was awake from her nap. Since she didn't trust the elevator in the apartment she rushed out the door, down the buildings' hallway stairs to the first floor of the duplex. She stayed for a few minutes and played with the baby. By the time she got back upstairs to the kitchen it was on fire (due to a faulty electrical system).

That afternoon the famous English director, his attractive wife, the very proper English nanny and the baby moved to a hotel suite overlooking Central Park. They remained there happily for the duration of their stay. His show was a great hit, but, alas, there were <u>NO House Seats</u> in my name.

Furnished Apartments

If you're coming to New York on a temporary basis you can get an apartment that is furnished soup-to nuts. Some of the more expensive properties even offer daily maid service and are month-to-month leases. Because of the temporary nature of this situation, these properties come and go quickly, so be prepared to act with speed. Also, since inventory is limited and you'll never find something that's exactly "your taste" just look for something clean and functional.

If you have no furniture, or you're not bringing anything with you there's always the option of rental furniture. The choices are very nice and the process is very simple. You just go to the showroom and point to what pieces you want. And presto, an entire apartment full of furniture comes delivered to your door within 48-hours.

The Importance of Window Guards

Millions of apartments in New York City are subject to window guard regulations. The New York Health Code states that building owners must provide window guards in every apartment that has children up to 11-years of age. The guards prevent windows from opening more than 4.5 inches.

All The News That's Fit to Print

The best way to keep current about what's going on in the real estate market is to read the Sunday New York Times and also review their website. A great way to get an overview of the market is to go to Open Houses on Sundays. They are primarily listed on www.nytimes.com. Also, go to Streeteasy.com, it is a compilation of all brokerages listings.

The scheduled Sunday Open Houses are also listed on these sites. Most listings include floorplans and photos to help you screen places in advance.

CHAPTER 3

Buying and Selling with Success

This can be a terrifying process. So many factors come into play. What appears to be the simplest transaction can become a nightmare. Here is some important information to guide you through the long and slippery road that is the New York real estate market.

Find a <u>Good Broker</u>

I just don't see how you can be involved in real estate in this city without a broker to guide you. There are so many technical details to get a deal done that it's really a necessity. This ironclad rule is in effect whether you're a buyer or a renter.

If you're a buyer, a broker can tell you instantly if you qualify for a coop. For example, in some of the more exclusive Fifth or Park Avenue properties, bloodline and your social standing is much more important than your actual bank account (although you'll need this as well). You need someone to represent you in contract negotiations and to work with the lawyers, the exclusive broker (this is the person representing the seller), the banks, mortgage broker, the building management and the Board of Directors. On every sales deal, no matter how big or small there is a cast of thousands to communicate with. The only way you would have time to do your own sale is to quit your day job and deal with all of these aforementioned players on a constant basis. The Board Package is its own nightmare. There is an art to putting this together and submitting it and this is where the broker really earns their commission.

If you're a seller and want to list your property yourself be prepared to hear from many brokers every day. You'll be faxing floorplans constantly, spending money on advertising, answering questions, and showing the apartment. Sometimes you'll be stood up by a no-show broker and customer. In addition to all of the above, negotiating for yourself is a very tricky situation. **Case in point: I just completed a deal on a property I represented with two shark brokers vying for a property. I barely escaped with my life. My seller was so upset with all of the shenanigans she offered to pay me more just to make it go away.**

My point is that unless you have a lot of spare time on your hands you don't want to be a buyer or a seller without a good broker to guide you through the labyrinth of the NYC real estate market.

How to Be a Successful Buyer

Now you know that your first order of business is to find a broker you feel comfortable working with. If you're new in town and have nobody to ask about a referral then go to www.nytimes.com—The New York Times Internet site. Do a search with your specific criteria and make appointments with the exclusive brokers to see some apartments. You'll most likely meet a broker you are comfortable with during your viewings and you'll be able to work with that person. My advice is to work with a large company because you can be certain they have all the listings. They'll be able to get you in to see everything.

Manhattan does not have Multiple Listings as it exists in other major markets. We have something similar called co-brokering. This insures that you will get to see all the appropriate properties on the market just like with the Multiple Listings Service. Here's how it works: A broker gets an "exclusive" on a property. Your broker can show you the property by calling the exclusive broker and making an appointment. This is why it's important to work with a broker from a major agency in town. We all co-broke with each other and share listings, but if you're with a larger firm your broker will probably get a call back quicker. And speed, getting access quickly to a hot listing is the way to get what you want. So, be sure to work with a major firm.

Another way to find a broker is to go to Open Houses. Interview them about the market their experience and see who you feel comfortable with. Since you'll be spending a lot of time with this person make sure you like them, trust them and feel confident in their abilities. I don't recommend using more than one broker at a time for the following two reasons. First, every major firm has the same listings so your broker can show you everything. However, if you are losing respect for the broker after a certain amount of time has gone by, then switch to someone else. Second, there is nothing more upsetting to a broker who is working hard on your behalf than to call an exclusive broker and register your name to see their property, only to find out you've already seen the property through someone else. When it happens to me I am not happy. I hate to be "cheated on" and I make my displeasure known to my customer. It is very disheartening and demoralizing. It puts a layer of negativity on your relationship with your broker. If your broker is on the ball they will show you all the properties in your category. They are not hiding listings from you.

If you are searching on the Internet and see something advertised through another broker, just contact your agent and ask them about it. This loyalty will inspire even harder work on the part of your broker. It will be a win-win situation for you.

As far as etiquette is concerned, I feel the buyer or renter should pay for cabs. You are taking up a broker's time—and after all, we only have our time. This is a nice touch, not that expensive in the scheme of things and it will endear you to your broker forever.

Getting Pre-Qualified For A Mortgage

It is important to meet with a mortgage broker and get a letter saying you qualify for a mortgage—along with the amount you can borrow. Also, a broker has to qualify you for the building, especially for a coop. You'll have to be comfortable giving a broker a sketch of your financials. Brokers may ask you to fill out what's called a REBNY form so they can see your assets, liabilities, and how much cash and marketable securities you have.

The Bidding Process

If and when your search has yielded something you want, you're ready to make a bid. Depend on your broker for guidance. They will test the waters by having a heart to heart, broker to broker discussion with the listing agent. Your broker may be able to find out if there have been any offers and what the board is like. In my opinion the key to negotiating is not wanting something so badly that you get into bidding wars (sometimes involving sealed bids). Pick a number you are comfortable with and stop there. Don't get involved in the feeding frenzy. Be willing to let the apartment go.

Meeting of the Minds

Let's say you and the seller come to a meeting of the minds and you are going forward with the deal. In New York only signed and fully executed contracts are binding. So now the rush is on. This is where everyone involved in the deal needs to swing into action. This comprises you and your broker, the listing broker, the buyer and sellers lawyers, and the mortgage broker. It is imperative to find a good real estate lawyer. Your broker will be able to guide you with this. You've got to get the contract signed as soon as possible because without your signature and the seller's on the contract, plus your 10% deposit, you can lose the apartment. The listing broker has a fiduciary responsibility to the seller to continue showing the apartment until there is a fully executed contract.

The Building's Financials

The first thing your lawyer will do prior to you signing the contract is to look at the most recent Financial Statement for the building, as well as read the coop board meeting minutes. This will determine if the building has unexpected issues such as lawsuits, planned renovations—all which could raise the monthly maintenance. These statements are usually released in April or May for the prior year. According to real estate attorney Keith Schuman (212) 490-0100, it is important to review the last two years of financials to track changes in income, expense and reserves.

The building's financials statement is usually prepared by a CPA and will show if the building is in good or poor financial condition. A financial statement should include a balance sheet describing assets and liabilities, a statement of income and expenses (also known as a statement of operations) and a statement of cash flows. Footnotes are used to clarify many of the numbers that appear in the statement and will disclose other pertinent financial information.

According to Mr. Schuman there are three major areas to focus on when reviewing financial statements: assets, income and expenses. If the building is a co-op, the status of the underlying mortgage is also very important. The "assets" section of the financial statement should reflect what amount of cash and/or reserve fund is held by the apartment corporation or condominium. The cash on hand is the amount of uninvested money held by the apartment corporation or the condominium at the end of the year.

The reserve fund generally consists of monies that have been invested and is used for repairs or capital improvements to the building. However, the board may have other reasons to utilize these funds. For example, if an underlying mortgage is to be refinanced, these funds may be used to pay for the expenses incurred in refinancing.

The general rule followed by accountants is that the reserve fund should equal one-third of the annual maintenance income. This rule may be unrealistic if the building expects to make major repairs or improvements. Many cooperative reserve funds are replenished by income received from the "flip tax", a charge levied by the building when units change hands. Ask your realtor if the building you are considering has a flip tax—and who pays it, the buyer or the seller.

Next, the attorney looks at the "statement of income and expenses" section of the financial statement. It will indicate whether or not the apartment corporation receives maintenance or common charge payments in excess of the operating expenses. If it does, the result will be a cash surplus to the building. If it does not, the result will be a deficit. This shortfall may be offset with monies received from flip taxes, sublet fees, interest income from reserve funds, laundry income and commercial rent, if any. If operating expenses exceed maintenance charges or common charges, even with the monies to help offset expenses, it is most likely that maintenance or common charges will be increased to cover the shortfall, or a special assessment may be charged to all unit owners or shareholders.

Most co-ops operate on a fiscal year ending on December 31st. It is important that the financial statements be available in the early part of the following year, no later than the beginning of May.

Another warning sign to look for are uncollected maintenance charges and unpaid bills. If uncollected maintenance is in excess of 5-percent of the total annual maintenance charges for the building, there are serious problems in the building. This is a sign that nobody is paying attention to cash flow in the building and there is no system in place for collections. Unpaid bills should not be in excess of 5-percent of the total maintenance either.

One of the most important issues in deciding to purchase a cooperative apartment, according to Keith Schuman, Esq. is the status of the building's underlying mortgage. A majority of apartment corporations will own their building with one or more mortgages usually held by an institutional lender. It is very important to make a determination as to what type of mortgage exists, how many mortgages there are and when they will mature.

The details of the underlying mortgage are usually found in the footnotes section of the financial statement. If the mortgage is maturing soon, it will most likely have to be refinanced at a significant expense to the apartment corporation, unless it is such a small amount that the shareholders can absorb paying off any principle balance remaining at maturity. A long-term mortgage is more favorable to a shareholder since there will not be a risk locating a new lender and incurring a large expense in a short time period. If the underlying mortgage is maturing soon, it may be difficult to locate a lender to provide a co-op loan to an individual purchaser. Many lenders require a minimum of two years to be left on the underlying mortgage.

Mr. Schuman goes on to say that if the rate is adjustable, the monthly installment may fluctuate, possibly causing maintenance to increase. Another important issue is whether monthly installments are applied to interest only, or if the payment is "amortized." If the mortgage is amortized, a portion of the monthly payment is utilized to reduce the principal balance of the loan. If the payments are applied to interest only, at maturity the entire principal balance will have to be refinanced. When an unamortized loan matures, it may mean the apartment corporation will have to refinance the entire principal balance at a higher interest rate which may result in an increase of maintenance.

It is also important to determine whether there are existing property tax abatements on the building and when they expire. When this happens property taxes increase and so do your monthly maintenance charges. Also, determine the number of unsold unit in the building and the projected major repairs. This information can generally be found in the Notes of the Financial Statement.

If there are too many unsold units or rentals in the building, some lenders might object to lending in the building. "Unsold units" are apartment still owned by the original sponsor, the sponsor's designees or investors.

And if major repairs or improvements are being planned, the estimated cost of these repairs should be determined as well as whether the reserve fund has sufficient money to pay for them. If not, it could mean an unexpected assessment for the buyer.

Mr. Schuman says that a buyer should try to accompany his lawyer when he goes to examine the minutes of the building's board of directors, which covers two years of meetings. This will help them find out information that might not be included in the financial statement. This includes information about tax abatements and future repairs, and gives you an overall idea about additional issues that are important in the building.

If there is a commercial lease, find out the terms of their leases. This is very important because, once again, your maintenance could be affected.

If there is a lot of pending litigation or huge legal fees this could be another red-flag. Well run buildings don't have this kind of negative activity. Once again, look in the footnotes of the financial statement for this information.

A condominium does not have an underlying mortgage on the building. However, if the sponsor owns numerous apartments in the building, the cost of the real estate taxes and common charges on those units, along with any mortgage debt he may have could exceed any income (i.e. rent) he may receive on those units. If he can no longer meet his expenses and fails to pay common charges, it will have a negative effect on the running of the building. Most financial statements do not disclose how many apartments a sponsor owns or whether the income he receives exceeds his expenses. The information is an amendment to the offering plan and should be closely examined.

Mr. Schuman says financial statements are usually finalized and released to shareholders between March and May if the fiscal year ends on December 31. If you purchase a co-op in February, March or April the financials can be over 14-months old and many numbers may have changed. For example, it is possible that an underlying mortgage in a co-op may have been refinanced within this time period. The managing agent of the co-op or condo will usually provide updated information. Other areas to be examined to determine the financial strength of a building are: maintenance or common charge history; whether there are or have been assessments and for what reasons; whether there are real estate tax abatements and what the taxes will be when the abatement expires; the number of apartments that are sponsor or investor owned; what repairs have been made or will be made in the building; whether there is a flip tax, if there is pending litigation against the co-op or condo; and when commercial leases that bring income to the building expire.

Mortgage Contingency Clauses

This is a clause that allows the buyer to cancel a deal if they are not able to obtain a mortgage. If you are a buyer your lawyer will probably insist on this clause because it can protect you. In a hot market however, when there are multiple bids, you usually have to waive this clause. The truth is that even though you obtain a mortgage commitment from a lender you can still lose your deposit if you are unable to get the loan. Sometimes a lender changes their mind and they don't give the loan even after they've given you a commitment. This can happen for a variety of reasons. Perhaps the borrower's financial circumstances change and they are unable to come up with the closing costs. Or the buyer loses their job or incurs some type of debt after the commitment is given but prior to the closing on the apartment. These are things for you, as the borrower, to look out for when getting a mortgage. Remember that any negative change in financial circumstances can lead to your loan being revoked.

In addition, mortgage commitments are contingent on the appraisal of the property. This is why it is so important to make certain that the mortgage contingency clause is still in effect while the appraisal is being done. If the mortgage contingency expires prior to the appraisal being done, and you haven't gotten an extension, there can be a major problem if the appraisal is less that what the lender wants to see. This leads to serious difficulties for the buyer because the property is worth less than you agreed to pay and the lender does not want to finance it.

When a lender gives you a pre-approval for a mortgage, it is only qualifying the borrower, not the building. But the building must qualify as well. For example, trouble can arise if a building has less than 10-units, in buildings where the bank has already made loans to 25-percent of the cooperative shareholders and in buildings with financial problems.

Mortgages

Once you have an executed contract you will now apply to get a mortgage commitment. Because of the rapidly changing mortgage rates and the new products on the market, many people choose to work with a mortgage broker to find the right financing product for them. I have found, through personal experience that in many cases the mortgage brokers have better rates than the banks themselves.

You will need to fill out an extensive loan application listing assets and liabilities (credit card bills, car loans for example). This includes W-2 statements and paystubs if you are salaried; two years of tax returns and YTD profit and loss statement if you are self-employed. Also needed are stock brokerage/IRA/401K accounts, three months bank statements stock and mutual fund accounts.

The bank will send out an appraiser to estimate the fair market value of the property. They look at the property and compare it to recent sales of comparable apartments for an accurate value.

The Board Package for a Co-Op

Once your attorney gives the okay to sign the contract and put the 10-percent deposit in the seller's attorney's escrow account, it is time to start putting together the board package. You must disclose detailed financial information about yourself in order to prove your financial ability to afford the apartment. There are no strict formulas regarding what buildings are looking for in terms of cash assets. Some buildings are tougher than others. This is an important part of the deal your broker can help you with. When filling out your net worth statement you must provide backup documents proving the money you say you have actually exists. Be prepared to include several monthly bank and stock statements with your package. There are also social and business reference letters required. The reason for all this detailed information is that co-ops use it as a way of protecting the shareholders from those who do not fit the financial and social profile of the building.

Give the board everything they require and disclose exactly what it is asking for. Don't submit information piecemeal. Be neat and give them everything at once. Don't edit out pages on your tax returns and don't add zeros to your net worth. Some boards require that a net-worth statement is signed by an accountant before you submit it. If you are selling another property don't forget to tell this to the board. Include a signed contract, or at the very least, the broker's marketing material to prove it is for sale. This will show that you have less debt than it might seem initially. Make sure that the numbers are consistent. The loan application, the net worth affidavit and the financial statements should all be in sync. Everything needs to add up, with all the back-up to your claims in place.

One thing people mistakenly leave out of their financial statement is the 10-percent deposit for the apartment which is in the seller's attorney's escrow account. So don't forget to include it in your net worth statement. Make your package as neat and as easy to understand as possible. Include everything the instructions ask for. If the board requires three-personal reference letters, don't submit two. This is very important. Boards take their job very seriously and they want what they want. Problem areas for high-end buyers may be: money that is too new, reference letters from people who aren't high enough on the totem pole, large salaries but not enough assets to back it up, New York as a second residence, overseas assets and parents buying for their children.

The coop board package cannot be submitted until the buyers get the mortgage commitment which can take four weeks. When everything is in order and the required paperwork is in place your broker will submit multiple copies to the Managing Agent of the building for their examination. They in turn review it and once they are satisfied with the contents they will pass your package on to the board members. Once the board reviews your package they may have questions, which could require additional financial information or a letter explaining your particular situation. This process can take an additional month or more after the mortgage commitment is received. So there can be at least two months between the contract signing and board approval where both the buyer and seller are in limbo.

What Assets Co-op Boards Want to See

The board looks at your assets and determines the buyer's ability to meet his financial obligations. There aren't any standard formulas but all boards want to see a cushion to make them comfortable that you can afford the apartment. Some boards want the buyer to have a reserve equal to or more than the apartment is selling for. Some fancier buildings want assets that are multiples of the apartments selling price. For example, a Fifth Avenue building might want the buyer's net worth to be at least double the purchase price. In less restrictive buildings, boards are not as concerned with net worth as they are in your monthly income. They look for a monthly income about three times the combination of the buyer's maintenance and debt service.

The Co-Op Board Meeting

When board members are satisfied with your ability to financially afford the apartment and monthly maintenance they will set up a board interview. Dress conservatively and in the meeting don't ask a million questions. Remember, nobody ever got rejected for being boring. Just be low key, pleasant and professional looking. They don't want to accept somebody involved in litigation so be careful of your answer if this subject comes up. A good way to ingratiate yourself is to offer to serve on one of their committees. However, do not say you want to run for the board. Just be sedate and try to get out of there as soon as possible. Once you've made it to the meeting, you're on the way to being approved. Just don't act obnoxious or inappropriate and you shouldn't have trouble getting accepted.

Because a co-op is a private corporation, the courts will not challenge decisions made by the board. Co-op boards don't have to give a reason why they rejected your application. And discrimination is very difficult to prove.

There are instances where the board is not entirely happy with your financial picture and impose certain conditions upon a prospective shareholder. In some cases they want a guarantee from a relative or third party to ensure that maintenance fees are paid on time. But this individual has to meet certain financial requirements set by the board to be accepted as a guarantor. In other cases the board wants one to three years maintenance put in an escrow account to guarantee payment of the maintenance or common charges, if the building is a condo.

Condo Board Approval

The paperwork and approval process is much easier in this scenario. There is a board package to fill out which usually involves an application, your financial picture, and reference letters. In most cases, there is no board meeting. You are approved based on your application. The condo has a 21-day right of first refusal, but buildings very rarely exercise that right. This means that the building would have to buy the apartment if they turn you down. Unless you are a known terrorist or O.J. Simpson you should have no worries.

Timing

Once you've found the apartment you want, the entire procedure from contract signing to closing should take between eight to twelve weeks. There is a lot to do—between getting the mortgage, finding and interviewing contractors and decorators through to completing the board package, waiting for a Board interview, then waiting to hear if you've been accepted. It can take a day or a week or two to find out if you've passed the board interview. This is so frustrating for everyone concerned. But there is no rushing a board.

It's best to take a wait and see attitude, as difficult as this is. Realize that you have no control over the situation, take a deep breath and think good thoughts.

The Walk-Thru

Prior to the closing you do a walk-through of the apartment to be certain that everything is the way it was represented to you in your contract. However, most properties are sold in "as in" condition. Once you're satisfied that everything is okay, it's time to close. New York State is a "buyer beware" jurisdiction. So it is up to the buyer to conduct a reasonable inspection of the property before they sign the contract and again just before closing.

Closing Costs

All buyers and sellers should consult their own attorney and mortgage broker for more specific information on these charges. Some of the costs can be rolled into the mortgage.

The Closing

There is a cast of thousands at the closing. This includes the buyer, seller, the exclusive broker, the selling broker, the sellers and buyers attorneys', the buyers bank, the sellers bank and in the case of a coop, sometimes the Managing Agent. Certified checks are exchanged and closing documents are executed. After several hours of paperwork finally the deed (for a condo) or a stock certificate and proprietary lease (for a coop) are given to you. The apartment is finally yours. You've paid for it with blood, sweat and money. Congratulations!

How to be a Successful Seller

The first thing you need to concern yourself with is to determine the best way to sell your apartment. The choices are selling it yourself through advertising in The New York Times and various websites or calling a broker. In my opinion, the best and most efficient thing to do is to give a broker an exclusive.

The New York State Real Property Law states there are two types of exclusives. The first is called an "exclusive right to sell" and the second is an "exclusive agency". The "exclusive right to sell" law states the seller of a piece of property agrees to act only through the broker they have signed the agreement with. If there is any inquiry of offer from other brokers or buyers, the owner must refer them to their exclusive broker.

The law states that under the "exclusive agency" the seller can deal directly with prospective buyers who were not introduced to them by their exclusive broker, but not other brokers. No decent broker in this town will go along with this scenario. It is too much work and who wants to be competing against the owner.

Both of these agreements allow the exclusive broker to contact other brokers to help sell your property. But under "exclusive agency" the owner can sell the property themselves and not owe a broker's commission.

However, under the "exclusive right to sell" agreement, if a seller finds a buyer on their own the seller still must pay the commission to the exclusive agent, as long as this falls into the time that the exclusive agreement is in effect.

New York City brokers usually have to schedule all appointments to show a property through the listing (exclusive) broker, who then accompanies the co-broker (selling broker) and the customer to the property.

New York City is not affiliated with the multiple listings system. Our own version is called exclusive listings. It works as follows. A seller gives a broker an exclusive on their apartment, usually for 3 to 6-months. The exclusive broker is responsible for marketing the apartment through advertising, the broker's website as well as others such as Streeteasy.com and The New York Times, open houses (if allowed by the building) and by co-brokering (giving out the listing to all other New York City brokers). The commission you as the seller pays is 6% of the selling price, and if it is sold through a co-broke, each broker gets 3%.

Why Exclusives Work

Why do I think an exclusive is the best way to market your apartment? First, it will save you an incredible amount of time. If you call all the brokers in New York City to list your apartment yourself you will be bombarded with so many phone calls everyday you'll want to change your number. The brokers will have questions, want to preview or make an appointment to see the property, change or cancel an existing appointment, or just plain stand you up. You'll have to fax floorplans, building financials and have many time-consuming conversations. It is a full-time job, and an annoying one at that. An exclusive broker has a fiduciary responsibility to get you the best price for your property, something not always easy to do yourself.

Another benefit to having your own broker is to get the support of their marketing programs. Any top broker in the city will have a website that is accessed by millions of buyers all over the world, as well as visibility on other independent real estate websites. Your apartment will be featured with digital photos and a floorplan so that your place is being marketed literally 24-hours a day. In addition, there are ads in popular magazines and Open Houses. You can't get this kind of visibility yourself. This is free, just for giving a broker an exclusive. Advertising yourself can be a very expensive proposition week after week. Brokers have also pre-qualified their customers. They know if they are able to afford your apartment, whether they can get a mortgage and, most importantly, how to prepare the board package in order to be approved by your board to purchase the property.

How to Make a Quick and Profitable Sale

The most important aspect of selling an apartment is correct pricing. Brokers have other "comps" (comparable selling prices in your building and in similar apartments in the area). If you are interested in a quick sale do not overprice your apartment. One strategy some brokers use is to begin with a higher price, then see what the traffic will bear. If nothing happens after the first month or two of showings they lower the price. If your apartment is renovated with a new kitchen and bathroom it will sell more quickly than a similar place that is not redone. But, if it isn't already renovated before you put it on the market, now is not the time to put money into fixing it up.

Getting your apartment ready for sale is crucial. First, clean up. Empty out all closets, get rid of all clutter. If the paint is peeling, touch it up. If there is a leak fix it immediately. The cleaner, fresher, the nicer your apartment shows, the faster and better the offers become. Try really hard not to be home if the apartment is being shown. This isn't a comfortable scenario for anyone.

Usually the best offer is the first offer that you get. So, it is not wise to hold out for money if the offer is within the range you are looking for. Sometimes an apartment is really hot, gets multiple offers and the bidding prices goes to sealed bids. Prospective buyers give their best offer, including financing information and credit and coop board-worthiness. This scenario sometimes backfires. When people get out of the feeding frenzy mode they can have buyers remorse. They may decide it's too expensive or they feel they are overpaying. My point is, tread carefully before getting into this process.

After you and the buyer come to terms, including price, closing date and what fixtures are remaining, then your lawyer sends out a contract to the buyer's attorney. It should be signed and returned to your attorney with a ten-percent escrow deposit within five days. The seller signs the contract after the buyer signs it. Until it is countersigned by you, your broker will continue to show the property. If you get a better offer and you have not signed the contract you are not legally obligated to continue with the original deal. You are free to move on to deal number two, but proceed with caution. If everything is going well with deal number one it is not always in your best interest to dump that deal for a new, unknown situation.

Once the buyer has the signed contract in hand they can get a mortgage and begin putting together the board package. Your lawyer will make arrangements for all necessary parties to be at the closing such as your bank so you can pay off the existing mortgage.

Whether you're buying or selling, this process is very stressful. A good broker can help smooth the way. There is so much paperwork involved, between the banks, attorneys and boards—something is bound to go wrong. But at the end of it all you will hopefully have gotten what you want. E-mail me at heidiberger@mac.com if you have any questions. Best of Luck!

CHAPTER 4

NYC Neighborhoods

Manhattan Living and Culture

With a population of 1.6 million residing in an area of about 34 square-miles, Manhattan represents the epitome of big city life. Brimming with theaters, museums, restaurants, universities, quirky neighborhoods, and historic attractions, Manhattan is the ideal living choice for those who truly enjoy the urban lifestyle and the culture that comes with it.

The oldest and most densely-populated of the five boroughs of New York City, Manhattan is bounded by the Hudson River to the west and the East River on the east. Commonly divided into three different sections—Downtown (or Lower), Midtown, and Upper—Manhattan's streets are, for the most part, laid out in a strict grid plan, making it easy for even newcomers to navigate their way through the city's crowded streets.

Neighborhoods

Given Manhattan's diversity, neighborhoods within the borough are unique and fun to explore.

Many neighborhoods are associated with New York's so-called "Bohemian" subculture, created by the number of artists looking for their big break in the Big Apple. Neighborhoods rich with artistic influence include Greenwich Village, Alphabet City (made famous in the Broadway show "Rent"), the Lower East Side, and the East Village. These neighborhoods are complemented nicely by upscale areas such as: SoHo, the Upper East Side, and the Upper West Side, by far some of the wealthiest neighborhoods in the United States.

Other neighborhoods boast names that are indicative of those who've made their home there over the years. Little Italy, Chinatown and Koreatown are where most immigrants settled upon arriving from Europe and Asia. Chinatown is now home to one of the largest Chinese populations in America.

Harlem, having experienced a renaissance of sorts in the late 20th century, is benefitting from renewed interest and is home to numerous theaters and other arts centers.

Lifestyle

Those who live in Manhattan thrive on its fast pace and rich culture. Walking the streets of Manhattan is a common and necessary means of transportation, while public transportation also covers the entire borough and whisks riders to surrounding boroughs as well.

Manhattanites do, however, have at their disposal plenty of places to unwind and relax. Expansive Central Park, one of the largest city parks in the country, is spread over 843 acres and attracts some 35 million visitors annually, according to the NYC tourist bureau. Locals love it too and head there not only to walk, bicycle, skate, or jog, but also to enjoy the park's pretty lakes, visit the Central Park Zoo or Conservatory Garden, or take in a production at the Delacorte Theater.

Other areas of the city, like Lower Manhattan, have strived to provide as much green space as possible for local residents and, as such, have begun to attract young families with a desire to combine the convenience of city living with a healthy lifestyle for themselves and their children.

The Arts

No city in the U.S. boasts the wealth of arts–related activities than one can find in Manhattan. More than 40 large professional theaters line Broadway, providing locals and visitors with a choice of plays and musicals unrivaled anywhere else in the world. Each year, approximately $1 billion in tickets are sold for Broadway shows, and new and promising careers are constantly launched from the stages of its theaters.

Manhattan also boasts a huge concentration of art museums that boast prominent displays of artworks ranging from historic to contemporary. Museums of interest include the famous *Metropolitan Museum of Art*, *The Museum of Modern Art (MoMA)*, *American Museum of Natural History*, *The Whitney Museum of American Art*, *The Frick Collection*, and *The Guggenheim Museum*.

At least 75 other museums, large and small, are scattered throughout Manhattan and regularly provide locals with special programs for both adults and children, including workshops and even summer camps.

Dining

There are literally hundreds and hundreds of restaurants located in Manhattan, representing a wide variety of cuisine. Indeed, many of the world's top chefs have made the city their home and their eclectic restaurants attract foodies from around the globe.

However, the most enticing eateries in the city might just be the small mom–and–pop establishments that serve homemade food using fresh local ingredients. They are often the true gems of the Manhattan dining scene.

West Side

Lincoln Square

Lincoln Square is the Upper West Side residential neighborhood that surrounds Lincoln Center. At the heart of the Lincoln Center area is the largest performing arts complex in the United States. Stretching between West 62nd and 65th Streets from Columbus Avenue to Amsterdam, the complex covers more than 16-acres and hosts almost any cultural offering imaginable, from opera to film to musical theater, dance and everything in between. The busy street scene on any given day or night is a diverse mix of New Yorkers and visitors from all over the world; toward evening you'll find yourself among jazz lovers in cafes, film buffs making their way to Walter Reade Theater, checking concert schedules at Avery Fisher Hall and on their way to the Opera.

If that doesn't give you enough to do, Riverside Park lies only a few blocks to the west. There's a feeling of both classic and brand-new here. You'll find tree-lined storybook New York streets in the elegant, residential Upper West Side—home to so many families—with Central Park never far away. With its location close to Midtown, this is a great neighborhood for professionals. It's also a public transportation hub. Families can enjoy the best of the parks and great supermarkets from the vast Whole Foods market in the Time Warner Center to countless specialty delis and bakeries and enough restaurants to fit any budget or taste.

Morningside Heights

Morningside Heights is bounded by the Upper West Side to the south, Morningside Park to the east, Harlem to the north, and Riverside Park to the west.

With Broadway as its main thoroughfare and Columbia and Barnard Universities dominating the neighborhood, this area of the Upper West Side is always bustling with a diverse group of people. The University's main campus extends from 114th to 120th Streets, and many residents are either students who come and go with school semesters or the original residents who have lived in this neighborhood for most of their lives. The surrounding area is peaceful and serene, close to (express) mass transit and a quick trip to midtown.

In recent years this neighborhood has become even more of a vibrant and lively community. Many restaurants, bars, and coffee shops have brought their businesses here, drawing crowds on any given day and motivating other business owners to consider this the newest extension of the Upper West Side. Several of the city's most impressive landmarks, such as the Episcopal Cathedral of Saint John the Divine and the Riverside Church can be found here, and Claremont Avenue, which runs north for several blocks from 116th Street, is one of the most attractive residential streets in the City. Blessed by major parks and good architecture, Morningside Heights experienced a wave of gentrification in the mid-1980's, especially around Broadway, that has continued since.

Upper West Side

Manhattan's Upper West Side, backdrop of Woody Allen movies and Seinfeld, is one of the City's most desirable—and livable—neighborhoods for anyone seeking the classic New York City lifestyle. In addition to the 16-acres of the world-class cultural mecca that is Lincoln Center, there's Central Park, the Midtown business district and the area's treasured residential addresses. The development of the Time Warner Center at Columbus Circle and the extension of Riverside Park along the Hudson River have made the area even more of an ideal place to come home to. A longtime classic neighborhood for New Yorkers, the Upper West Side is home to celebrated restaurants like Jean Georges, the famed H & H bagels and Zabar's delis, and arguably the best educational facilities, community centers and museums in the City.

The Upper West Side offers the best of the City; from the spectacular views of the Hudson and uninterrupted rows of distinctive pre-war apartment buildings on West End Avenue/Riverside Drive to the breathtaking park vistas visible from the some of the City's most elegant addresses on Central Park West. The vibrant neighborhood of Lincoln Square and Broadway, lined with supermarkets, cafés, bookstores, fine restaurants and boutiques, only add to this area's appeal as there is something for everyone who lives here. In addition, service by almost all subway lines—and Midtown just to the South—guarantees that it's a short commute to anywhere in Manhattan.

East Side

Carnegie Hill

Located between 79th and 98th Streets and Fifth Avenue and Third Avenues, the Upper East Side neighborhood known as Carnegie Hill is, for many New Yorkers with families, the city's finest—if not quintessential—residential neighborhood. The area gets its name from the great mansion and fenced garden—now the National Design Museum—that the steel magnate built on Fifth Avenue between 90th and 91st Streets.

While busy Lexington Avenue near 90th Street offers the classic selection of chain stores, gourmet delis and eyewear boutiques, location dictates that these be interspersed with progressive preschools, sushi restaurants, and that venerable cultural anchor, the 92nd Street Y. Cross-streets are lined with elegant brick towers and stately pre-war townhouses.

The existence of historic landmark districts and very active community groups guarantees that new developments here will have to proceed with care. The neighborhood boasts the city's highest concentration of major museums—the "Museum Mile"—including the crown jewel that is the Metropolitan Museum of Art—as well as fine schools, numerous religious institutions, and a large supply of sizable apartments, mostly in pre-war buildings. There's also a healthy mix of distinguished architecture, good public transportation, and the coveted proximity to Central Park as well as a very pleasant collection of charming restaurants along Madison Avenue.

Roosevelt Island

Roosevelt Island is a narrow island in the East River. It lies between the boroughs of Manhattan and Queens, though it's considered part of the borough of Manhattan. Most of the buildings on the island are rental residences, though a co-op (Rivercross) and a luxury condo (Riverwalk Place) can be found here as well.

The island's residential community was developed as a car-free zone—the intent was that residents would park in a large garage and use public transportation to get around. Though automobile traffic has become common, many areas of the island remain car-free. Businesses like Starbucks and Duane Reade cater to residents as do a handful of restaurants and cafes, and there's a local branch of the New York Public Library. Roosevelt Island even has its own newspaper, the WIRE.

The island is accessible from the rest of the city using the Roosevelt Island Tramway or the 63rd Street subway line and an MTA bus route runs between the island and Astoria. The Octagon—a 500-unit luxury building—in addition to the aforementioned Riverwalk condominium, has brought an influx of young residents to the island, making this a more desirable neighborhood option for families and others who want convenience and more space at lower prices than they'd find across the river in Manhattan.

Upper East Side

The Upper East Side is known for being New York's—possibly the country's—most elegant residential neighborhood, with streets near Park and Fifth Avenues conveying the hushed ambiance of the privileged and powerful. The majority of apartment buildings here were built between the turn of the century and the 1930s.

Fifth Avenue is entirely residential in this area except for the many cultural institutions along its "Museum Mile," home to the City's highest concentration of cultural institutions including the Metropolitan Museum of Art, the MoMA, Whitney, and Guggenheim museums, the Frick Collection and many smaller high-quality institutions. Also here are the elegant residential enclaves of Sutton and Beekman Place. Carnegie Hill is the City's most coveted neighborhood for families, and Yorkville toward the East River is a popular home to young professionals and singles who enjoy stunning river views and the added perk of Carl Schurz Park.

Central Park, on the western border of this area, makes a world-class front yard—with its zoo, tennis courts, formal gardens, bridle paths, running tracks and reservoir. Madison Avenue—possibly the world's most famous retail address and famed center of the advertising industry in the mid-20th century—entices shoppers with boutiques like Chanel, Prada, Tiffany and fashion mecca Barney's New York, and a more commercial strip runs through the southeast corner, anchored by Bloomingdale's at 59th Street and Lexington/Third Avenues.

World-class hotels in the neighborhood include the Carlyle, the Mark, the Lowell and the Plaza-Athene, and dozens of fine restaurants line side streets. Transportation includes a number of buses and subway stations at 77th, 68th and 59th Streets on Lexington Avenue, 60th Street on Fifth Avenue, as well as plentiful taxicab service due to the area's aforementioned hotels.

Upper Manhattan

East Harlem

East Harlem/El Barrio (Spanish Harlem) stretches from First Avenue to Fifth Avenue and from East 96th Street to East 125th Street.

The diverse neighborhood offers a wide range of choices for anyone looking for a new home among a choice of row houses, new condos, studios, lofts and brownstones. Space is more plentiful here, and outdoor gardens and parking—extremely rare elsewhere in Manhattan—are a frequent and pleasant surprise. New buildings offer stunning views of the East River and the two East Side uptown bridges.

The area is a find for lovers of foods from all over the world as well. From pizza to Creole and Indian, you'll probably find it here. New restaurants and shops have arrived, too, though cultural legends endure—the neighborhood still celebrates the City's first Italian feast honoring Our Lady of Mount Carmel. East Harlem is also home to Metropolis, one of the few major television studios north of Midtown as well as a number of museums and cultural centers.

The newly-opened East River Plaza on 116th Street and FDR Drive has brought megastore convenience (Target, Best Buy, Marshall's) to the area as well. A Metro-North Railroad Station at 125th Street, a 4-5-6 Lexington Avenue subway stop, and an entrance to the FDR Drive make this an access-friendly area.

Hamilton Heights

The Harlem neighborhood at the center of West 125th Street to West 155th Street, from Riverside Drive to St. Nicholas and Edgecombe Avenues is known as Hamilton Heights.

It is best known for "Strivers' Row," consisting of some of the most beautifully restored historic townhouses in New York City, many with painstakingly renovated ornate staircases, fireplaces, pocket doors, and moldings. The stunning block of homes overlooks gardens in the back and offers the added value of subway access (with stops at 135th and 145th Streets). These beautiful row houses are the best known, but overall this is a neighborhood with an unusually high concentration of historic single-family homes built in a variety of notable architectural styles ranging from Beaux-Arts to Romanesque.

Some more great reasons to call this neighborhood home are Riverbank State Park, the City College Campus of the City University of New York, St. Nicholas Park and access to the Hudson River as well as future plans that include state-of-the art environmental design and public art. Restaurants and nightlife in the area include many new and old favorites including a revamped version of the legendary El Morocco nightclub. Nearby, the neighborhoods of Inwood and Washington Heights are rich in culture and natural beauty with Fort Tryon and Inwood Hill Parks offering acres of unspoiled land and river views.

Harlem

Harlem and Central Harlem is located west of Fifth Avenue and the East River and stretches from 110th Street, or Central Park North, to 155th Street.

Harlem has long been defined by boom-and-bust cycles and dramatic population shifts. In the 1920s and 1930s, the neighborhood was the center of the first Harlem Renaissance, a cultural high point in the history of the American black community. In the late part of the 20th century, Harlem experienced a massive building boom. Newer buildings range in size and style from studios to lofts and luxury condos. Harlem boasts many of the finest original townhouses in New York.

There are a growing number of shopping options on 125th Street, and in addition to Central Park, Marcus Garvey Park offers twenty acres of play-space, concerts and events—like the City's Charlie Parker Jazz Festival—between 120th and 124th Streets. Iconic venues like the Apollo Theater draw visitors from around the world. The New York Times recently reported that the population of "Greater Harlem" had grown more since 2000—former U.S. President Bill Clinton moved into his Harlem office in 2001—than in any decade since the 1940s.

Harlem's newest population is refreshingly diverse, made up of residents who enjoy the neighborhood's history, the gorgeous homes and unrenovated gems, oozing with potential. Subways include the 6 for East Harlem; the 2 or 3 for Central Harlem; and the A, B, C, or D for West Harlem.

Hudson Heights

Hudson Heights—previously known as Fort Tryon—is within the boundaries of a larger area known as Washington Heights. It is bounded to the north by Fort Tryon Park, to the west by the Hudson River, to the east by Broadway and to the south by West 181st Street.

Manhattan's highest natural point (265 feet above sea level) is here, in Bennett Park. The neighborhood is mostly residential, with many pre-war buildings in the Art Deco, Art Nouveau, Neo-Classical, Tudor and

Gothic styles. Most are co-ops, though there are condos and rentals available here as well.

In recent years Hudson Heights has become a sweet spot for buyers who don't want to leave Manhattan but want more space for their money. The area is known for its hills and the cliffs that are now Fort Tryon Park. Its best-known cultural asset is The Cloisters—located in Fort Tryon Park as well—where the Metropolitan Museum of Art exhibits its collection of medieval art among serene walkways, dramatic medieval architecture and leafy paths.

Near 181st Street is a cluster of restaurants and tiny bodegas, the usual coffee house staples as well as the four-screen Coliseum Cinema, which has the distinction of being the only movie theater above 125th Street in Manhattan. If you work in Manhattan, Hudson Heights (West 181st Street) is only five stops to Port Authority on the A line via express.

Inwood

Inwood and Washington Heights are Manhattan's two northernmost neighborhoods and a sweet spot for buyers who don't want to leave the Island but want considerably more space for their money.

Inwood begins at Dyckman Street and extends to the most northern tip of Manhattan. It was a rural area well into the early 20th century, and its hills, cliffs and green spaces feel worlds away from the urban bustle of the city below. Inwood Hill Park on the Hudson River is a largely wooded city park that contains caves, the last salt marsh in Manhattan, and the last natural forest standing on Manhattan Island. Parts of Fort Tryon Park and Highbridge Park lie along Inwood's southern border. For even more outdoor options there are Isham Park, Jacob Javits Athletic Field and Columbia University's 23-acre athletic fields.

The area's best-known cultural asset is The Cloisters—located in Fort Tryon Park—where the Metropolitan Museum of Art exhibits its collection of Medieval art among serene walkways, dramatic Medieval architecture and leafy paths. Artists from Inwood and the surrounding communities participate in the annual Uptown Arts Stroll each summer.

The uptown neighborhood is filled with varied food finds, and a number of hip restaurants, cafes, bars, upscale wine and food shops and galleries. Inwood is served by the 1 and the A subway lines, with Port Authority only 5 stops away (20 minutes or less) via express.

Washington Heights

Washington Heights is the Manhattan neighborhood just north of Harlem from 155th Street to Inwood up to Dyckman Street.

The area is known for its hills and the cliffs—a real change of scenery for Manhattanites. The neighborhood's best-known cultural asset is The Cloisters—located in Fort Tryon Park—where the Metropolitan Museum of Art exhibits its collection of Medieval art among serene walkways, dramatic Medieval architecture and leafy paths. You'll find plenty of parks here, including Bennett Park, Fort Tyron Park, Fort Washington Park and Riverfront Park. Artists from Washington Heights and the surrounding communities participate in the annual Uptown Arts Stroll each summer, and there are several branches of the New York Public Library.

Within Washington Heights is the community known as Hudson Heights, a residential neighborhood made up of mostly pre-war buildings in the Art Deco, Art Nouveau, Neo-Classical, Tudor and Gothic styles that has become a sweet spot for buyers who want considerably more space for their money. The New Balance Track and Field Center in the Fort Washington Avenue Armory maintains an Olympic-grade track, and mountain bike races take place in Highbridge Park in the spring and summer.

Washington Heights is a vibrant, neighborly community with plenty of food finds, and a number of upscale wine and food shops and businesses. Washington Heights is connected to New Jersey via the George Washington Bridge and the neighborhood is served by the C and the A subways, with Port Authority only 5 stops away via express.

Downtown

Battery Park City

Battery Park City is a planned community covering 92-acres at the southwestern tip of lower Manhattan, and is one of Manhattan's youngest neighborhoods. There are no walk-ups, brownstones or tenement buildings here, only modern luxury towers that are either condos or rentals. The Battery Park City Green Building Guidelines were among the first of their type, making it one of the "greenest" neighborhood developments anywhere in the United States.

Due to its somewhat remote location, this is truly a neighborhood of its own—the community infrastructure caters to residents' lifestyles, with a number of gyms, restaurants, parks, indoor tennis, racquetball and golf facilities.

The neighborhood is the site of the World Financial Center and numerous housing, commercial and retail buildings. A stunning skywalk connects Battery Park City to the famed Wintergarden and the rest of the city. If the Wintergarden is the neighborhood's heart, its soul is the Esplanade, a long strip of boardwalk along the West Hudson, perfect for biking, rollerblading and jogging, with plenty of seating and impressive views.

The north end of the site is occupied by Stuyvesant High School, one of the city's finest. The development has tremendous appeal for people who work downtown, but nearly all major subways are nearby. Battery Park City may have seen some awkward times, but on a summer day—with an outdoor concert at the yacht-filled North Cove Marina, sailboats in the harbor, the Statue of Liberty in the background and outdoor cafés filled with people—it seems clear that it has survived rather magnificently.

Chelsea

Located between Midtown and the West Village, Chelsea offers good public transportation and proximity to the Midtown office district as well as the many attractions of downtown. The neighborhood is full of surprises as a result of a confluence of changing development patterns.

A melting pot of people can be found in Chelsea and the area's architecture reflects that same diversity. The area above 23rd Street by the Hudson River is post-industrial, featuring the newly-opened High Line Park. To the south, between Ninth and Tenth avenues, mid-nineteenth century townhouses stand, some restored to single-family use. The white-tile portholed National Maritime Union Building—now the chic Maritime hotel—is a notable landmark. Another converted neighborhood relic is the Episcopal Church of the Holy Communion that once was home to the infamous Limelight Disco.

In the 1990's the neighborhood saw an influx of art galleries seeking less expensive space than was available in SoHo. In one of the most rapid transformations in the city's history, the neighborhood has become one of the world's centers of modern contemporary art, with over 370 art galleries.

Chelsea Piers, a major waterfront recreational facility, reintroduced many New Yorkers to the area. The Ninth Avenue food mecca, better known as The Chelsea Market, boasts an impressive collection of gourmet food stores and restaurants, and the zone extending south of 14th Street—known as the Meat-Packing District—is one of the city's busiest nightlife centers.

East Village

Located North of Houston and South of 14th Street, the East Village has more of a "downtown" bohemian street style than its West-side counterpart—most in evidence on St. Marks Place (Eighth Street between Second Avenue and Avenue A), and buildings here are typically older generation tenement-style apartments. Though iconic clubs like CBGB and Electric Circus have closed, the neighborhood was home to its punk, rock, and jazz musician and artist denizens for decades. The easternmost section was long known as Alphabet City (for Avenues A-D), and you can still find in it some of the old East Village flavor as longtime residents, old—and new-school bohemians, NYU students and young professionals drink and dine side by side in the area's many restaurants and bars.

Prices tend to be a bit lower toward the river, though development has been steady for some time. Tiny storefronts offering great treats compete with fine restaurants on the neighborhood's narrow, tree-lined streets, which are also lined with chic boutiques, cafes and quirky vintage shops. Tompkins Square Park, despite a past history of riots and drugs, is one of the City's loveliest, with a well-loved dog run that brings pups and their owners from the surrounding streets and beyond. As with all far-east-side neighborhoods, subways are a bit scarce: The F at First Avenue and the 4, 5, 6 subway lines are a ten-minute walk in some cases, though city buses run regularly on the avenues.

Financial District

Nicknamed "FiDi," to highlight its neighborhood appeal, Lower Manhattan has historically been—and still remains—the City's primary business district. The pall cast over Lower Manhattan by the terrorist attacks of September 11, 2001 was surprisingly short-lived because of the City and federal government's resolve to rebuild and entice residents and businesses to the area. Despite prolonged controversies over the design of a rebuilt Ground Zero, Lower Manhattan began to pulse with new activity as old—and bold—office buildings were converted to apartments and as TriBeCa boomed with dozens of new and architecturally innovative developments.

The South Street Seaport and the Brooklyn Bridge along the East River offer a good variety of shops, cafes, hotels and restaurants as well as regularly scheduled concerts, boat rides and other activities, which adds to its ability to attract an influx of new residents, putting Lower Manhattan well on its way to becoming a vibrant mixed-use community.

North of Wall Street and the South Street Seaport lie City Hall, the Civic Center and the courts around Foley Square, Chinatown and Little Italy—all within walking distance of the Financial District—as is the Hudson-side esplanade at Battery Park City, the major retail facilities at the World Financial Center and the many restaurants and nightlife spots of TriBeCa to the west. Though the area has obvious appeal for people who work in the district, nearly all major subways stop close by.

Flatiron District

At the crossroads of some of the City's most desirable residential neighborhoods, the park that anchors Union

Square is bounded by 14th Street to the south, Union Square West, 17th Street to the north, and Union Square East.

To the north, the Flatiron District—named for the narrow, corner-defining Flatiron building at the intersection of Fifth Avenue and Broadway—became one of the City's more exciting areas for technology, commerce and nightlife in the last century. The New School and New York University have a noticeable presence here as well. At the center of the square on any given day you'll find a colorful, ever-changing street scene of entertainers, eccentrics, merchants and city folk passing through or stopping to meet.

Union Square Park itself is also the home of the City's best farmer's market, which offers a full bounty of specialty, artisanal and other fresh local and regional foods year-round, four times weekly. During the winter holidays, the square hosts a seemingly endless holiday gift market. Surrounding the park are blocks of stores from chain favorites to an unrivaled collection of gourmet food stores like Whole Foods and Trader Joe's. The streets that surround the square are lined with restaurants that overflow each evening with an after-work crowd, but you'll find no shortage of spots to meet for a more intimate drink or coffee. The area is convenient to most of the City, served by the 4, 5, 6, L, N, Q, R, and W subway lines.

Gramercy—Union Square

Surrounding a small private park (buildings and brownstones actually facing the gated park have keys),

Gramercy—the entire neighborhood is an historic district—feels almost like a small village in the heart of the City. Despite its elaborate brownstones, Victorian style architecture that rivals the London originals and oversized, elegant apartments on quiet narrow streets, the neighborhood offers a diverse and vibrant nightlife in the form of city-renowned restaurants, live music and local late night bars and clubs in addition to the five-star Gramercy Park Hotel.

Add another star for central location: Bounded by 14th Street to the south, First Avenue to the east, 23rd Street to the north, and Park Avenue South to the west, Gramercy is within walking distance to the offices of Midtown, the shops of NoHo, SoHo and points south as well as the nightlife of the of East and West Village.

There are at least five subway lines within a short walk of the park. The nearby Flatiron District—named for the narrow, corner-defining Flatiron building at the intersection of Fifth Avenue and Broadway—became one of the City's more exciting areas in the last century. And Union Square is nearby, with its well-loved farmers' market and constant ebb and flow of colorful city life.

Greenwich Village—NoHo

The West Village and Greenwich Village stretch from 14th to Houston Street between the Hudson River and Broadway, with Sixth Avenue demarcating the two neighborhoods. Known as the birthplace of the Beat movement and the folk music scene of the 1960s, Greenwich Village was once the City's counter-culture capital—the list of artists and intellectuals who have made it their home and cultural center is impressive. Today's Village is home to celebrities, fashion luminaries and Wall Streeters who want to be near work as well as families and young singles. New York University covers a significant portion of the neighborhood as well. The neighborhood still possesses a strong sense of community identity.

The heart of Greenwich Village is Washington Square Park with its impressive Arch. Several high-rises and loft buildings have arrived—but classically beautiful brick townhouse apartments on quiet, tree-lined streets still define the residential areas of the Village, and the Lower Fifth Avenue area between 13th and 9th Streets is one of the City's most elegant stretches. Apartment prices remain high despite economic fluctuations; some say the Village is downtown's most desirable residential area. Subways are plentiful—A, B, C, D, E, F,V at West 4th Street or N, R at 8th Street—and easy to find.

Little Italy—Chinatown

Chinatown and Little Italy are two of New York's most well-known ethnic neighborhoods. Walking through the streets beneath the fire escapes of turn-of-the-century tenements, your senses are awakened by the sights, sounds, and smells of the Italian and Chinese cuisines and cultures emerging from restaurants and shops.

Little Italy extends north of Houston Street up Sullivan and Thompson Streets; small coffee shops and family restaurants—and their 21st century counterparts—tempt passersby to sample the homemade cooking. Visitors come here for authentic cuisine and a taste of old New York.

Chinatown starts on Canal Street with storefronts spilling onto the sidewalk and the art of negotiation being finessed over everything from "designer" handbags to electronics. Manhattan's Chinatown is one of the largest Chinese communities outside Asia. It is not unusual to enter a street where all signs are in Chinese and where the stores are run without any English-speaking representatives. You'll find the majority of dining choices along the narrow, winding Mott and Mulberry Streets just below Canal Street.

Little Italy hosts the San Gennaro festival and in February the Chinese New Year is celebrated with dragon dances, parades and other traditional ceremonies, and thousands of tourists, residents and visitors join in the festivities. Apartment prices vary from block to block, from some of the cheapest in the city to higher-priced dwellings drawing residents who love the desirable downtown location.

Lower East Side

The Lower East Side is located north of Houston and south of Division Street, between the East River and Bowery. Its richest legacy is the influx of immigrants that settled in the area during the first half of the 20th century and the mark these groups left on the neighborhood.

After years of neglect, the neighborhood has made a complete turnaround aided by investment and a renewed interest in the "downtown" lifestyle. Older buildings have been renovated and new ones have risen seemingly overnight. Pre-war walk-ups can now be found next to full-service luxury buildings and sleek, modern condominiums, high-end rentals and hotel towers. This cleaner, safer Lower East Side boasts a vibrant and diverse nightlife, with limitless options from hip bars to cabaret theaters and Indie rock venues, but it still retains a friendly downtown community atmosphere.

Apartment prices are somewhat cheaper here than in the neighboring East Village, but there are few subway stops—the F and J, M, Z, G lines stop along First Avenue and Delancey Street, respectively—in the area. The neighborhood's landmarks reflect its heritage: Eldridge Street Synagogue, the Louis Abrons Arts for Living Center and the Lower East Side Tenement Museum as well as the delightful Katz's deli, Yonah Shimmel Knish and Russ and Daughters food shops bring a taste of old New York to the hip fashion boutiques and restaurants that mark the area's recent metamorphosis.

SoHo—Nolita

South of Greenwich Village and west of Little Italy, SoHo (which stands for South of Houston) is a relatively small area bounded roughly by Broadway, the Hudson River, Houston and Canal Streets. Its primary residential properties are in the SoHo Cast Iron Historic District along West Broadway. In the 1960s, artists began to move into this formerly industrial area in search of inexpensive and spacious studios and housing. By the early '70s, the presence of so many artists led to the area's renaissance—the large loft spaces were dramatically restored, real estate values soared, and demand for space extended to other "undiscovered" areas nearby.

The tremendous popularity of the area took the City by surprise and soon the chic boutiques and galleries that catered to the art crowd were followed by international designers like Chanel and Prada and high-end housewares and furniture shops, a Barney's Co-op, an Apple store and apparel chains like Diesel and Camper. The neighborhood is now known for its world-class shopping—on weekends it becomes a bustling marketplace.

But there are still parts of the neighborhood where you'll find a relaxed, chic downtown atmosphere. Cobblestone streets, traditional restaurants and European-style coffee shops still delight local residents. The neighborhood's artist-anchored culture is held in place by cutting-edge galleries like Dietch Projects and the annual Art Parade which brings out the most creative SoHo pioneers as well as young newcomers.

TriBeCa

The Triangle Below Canal Street (TriBeCa) began to gain its reputation as a residential neighborhood in the 1970s, when artists arrived in search of less expensive accommodations and studio space. The area's unique industrial-age architecture of lofts, warehouses and market spaces—and the lifestyle of its residents—was a major influence on the popularity of "loft living" in the 1980s.

TriBeCa has since then become a sought-after neighborhood for anyone seeking—and willing to pay for—spacious living quarters in an urban setting. Developers have converted many of the original warehouse buildings into luxury condos—including 101 Warren, 200 Chambers, Pearline Soap Lofts and 145 Hudson—and rentals.

The neighborhood's historic, loft-lined streets are relatively quiet after business hours save the buzz and glow of fine dining establishments, neighborhood bistros and cafes that keep residents' sophisticated palates happy. Thankfully missing are the frat bars and watering holes that are unavoidable in many of the City's residential areas. The TriBeCa Film Festival brings cinephiles and industry types from around the globe, and the addition of a 92nd Street Y outpost has given residents and their families a cultural hub. Shopping is plentiful as well, with small shops run by local and international designers and enough drug stores and delis to serve residents in standard Manhattan fashion.

Subway stops: The 1 or 2 line to Canal, Franklin, or Chambers Streets, or the A, C, E line to Canal or Chambers Streets.

West Village—Meat Packing District

The West Village and Greenwich Village stretch from 14th to Houston Street between the Hudson River and Broadway, with Sixth Avenue demarcating the two neighborhoods.

The West Village is home to celebrities and fashion luminaries as well as families and young singles wishing to lead a fairly low-key life behind elegant brick facades.

Several high-rises and loft buildings including the rippling facade of One Jackson Square and Richard Meier's tower at 173-176 Perry Streets contrast with classically beautiful brick townhouse apartments—including a handful of notable restored carriage-houses—yet still manage to make the neighborhood feel warm and welcoming and define the residential areas of the West Village.

A distinct European flair pervades tiny cafes and shops among the jumble of winding, tree-lined streets. Some of the City's finest restaurants are here as well. Apartment prices remain high despite economic fluctuations: Some say the West Village is downtown's most desirable residential area, and its future is sure to be reinforced by the emergence of many architectural projects along the High Line just to the north in Chelsea. Subways—A, B, C, D, E, F,V at West 4th Street or N, R at 8th Street are convenient to Village residents as well.

Midtown

Beekman

Two of the city's most sought-after residential addresses, Sutton Place and Beekman Place comprise the neighboring enclaves of elegant—though not overwhelmingly so—buildings along the East River, east of First Avenue with Midtown to the west. With dramatic views of the Queensboro Bridge and Roosevelt Island and easy access to the F.D.R. Drive, these neighborhoods are tiny oases of calm and community amid hectic Midtown commerce.

Sutton Place benefits from two public parks. One Sutton Place South—a neo-Georgian style mansion—is one of the city's grandest addresses. Two townhouse rows—between 57th and 58th Streets—share a large communal garden overlooking the East River.

Beekman Place runs from 49th to 51st Streets, consisting of two blocks of ivy-covered townhomes and co-op buildings. The neighborhood was named for the Beekman family, which built its mansion, Mount Pleasant, there in 1764. The grand apartment house at One Beekman Place was built in 1929, setting the tone for the little street. One Beekman Place opens directly to the river, and its south facade overlooks the United Nations and its gardens.

Though the area is a bit far from the nearest subway on Lexington and Third Avenues, an upside is that housing prices tend to be below those of the Upper East Side. The neighborhood boasts plenty of retail activity, including the vast Bridgemarket Food Emporium just below the Queensboro Bridge. Sutton East Tennis Club, an enclosed winter tennis facility, is another convenient amenity for neighborhood residents.

Central Park South

The residential area of Central Park South is small, but it offers what may be the City's most unrivaled views of Central Park, framed by the uptown city skyline. The apartments here are prewar residences, condos and co-ops, including a few available within classic hotels like the Plaza and the Ritz-Carlton. The cultural offerings of Lincoln Center, fine dining of

Columbus Circle and the shops at Time Warner Center are all nearby. The proximity of the corporate canyons of Midtown and nearby access to most of the City's subway lines makes almost all of Manhattan accessible in minutes. You'll find a collection of classic dining and gathering spots here as well, with Sarabeth's Restaurant and the Oak Room among the favorites.

Of course, there's the distinction of having Central Park for a backyard (or a front yard as the case may be). A perfect foil for the busy city, the park's 800+ acres offer any activity you can imagine—including miles of jogging and bike trails, playgrounds, ponds, athletic fields, a boathouse, zoo, wildlife conservatory, skating rink and much more—and plenty of fields, gardens and open spaces perfect for doing nothing at all. Central Park hosts concerts, theater performances, movie screenings, and countless other cultural events year-round as well.

Clinton

Clinton (also called Hell's Kitchen to reflect its colorful past), located in Midtown West, runs from 34th to 57th Street, from Eighth Avenue to the Hudson, and is the area's residential jewel. Midtown is the city's main business hub—a powerful magnet for shopping, entertainment and tourism.

What was once a run-down district has become a truly vibrant residential community. Valued for its proximity to Midtown, Clinton is home to a mix of young professionals, longtime residents, actors, artists and other entertainers who treasure the proximity to the nearby Times Square Theater District (the Clinton

Community Garden was created here by actors living in the area). Ninth Avenue is lined with low-key bars, restaurants—the avenue is known for its varied eateries—and shops. Galleries have opened, leading some residents to boast that the neighborhood may be "the next SoHo, without the attitude."

Southern neighbor Chelsea provides cultural, shopping and nightlife options as well. Worldwide Plaza at Eighth Avenue and 49th Street brought professionals to the area with attractive outdoor plazas as well as top-notch office space. The "green" Hearst Tower at 56th Street and Eighth Avenue is the newest headline-stealing architectural addition. Rockefeller Center and two of the city's three most important transportation gateways, the Pennsylvania/Long Island Rail Road station and the Port Authority of New York and New Jersey Bus Terminal, are located within blocks, making travel to just about anywhere convenient.

Fashion Center

Bordered by Fifth and Ninth Avenues from 34th to 42nd Street, the Fashion District (also called the Garment District) welcomed the 20th century as the center for fashion design and manufacturing and still retains its status as the fashion capital of the United States. While most actual clothing manufacturing has left Manhattan, there are still dozens of fabric shops in the Fashion Center—most can be found on 39th and 40th Streets between Seventh and Eighth Avenues. These cater mainly to the apparel industry, but dedicated retail shoppers can still drive a hard bargain.

The neighborhood has undergone tremendous change over the last decade, and the dynamic hub is now becoming its own diverse residential community. A still-growing neighborhood, the district has recently seen the arrival of a number of new residential towers and low-rise condos. The biggest draw is a convenient location in the heart of Midtown West, near office towers, lunch spots, restaurants and retail stores amid the bustling hive of Times Square.

Add to this an international influx of shoppers looking for bargains at Macy's in Herald Square—and F.I.T. students hoping to join the next wave of fashion superstars—for a big dose of being where the action is. The Fashion Center is in easy walking distance to many of the City's major transportation hubs like Pennsylvania and Grand Central Station as well as Madison Square Garden, making it easy to find both entertainment and escape.

Kips Bay

Named after Dutch settler Jacobus Henderson Kip, the neighborhood came to be associated with the vintage mid-20th century high-rise apartment and condominium complexes that anchor its skyline, including the 1,112 unit I.M. Pei-designed Kips Bay Towers.

Along Kips Bay's First Avenue corridor, the NYU College of Dentistry and School of Medicine, Bellevue Hospital Center and the Manhattan VA Hospital call the neighborhood home, as does a small population of medical students and professionals who live nearby.

In addition to the medical professionals who call the neighborhood home, Kips Bay is known for having some of the more affordable housing options. To accommodate this residential community, Kips Bay Plaza was built in the late '90s and boasts an AMC/Loews movie theater, a Borders bookstore, a Crunch gym and a 24-hour Rite Aid. You'll find a growing collection of restaurants and cafes for casual and fine dining as well as a small cluster of bars and pubs catering to young singles. Nearby landmarks like the Empire State Building and the United Nations add to the feeling of being in a very "New York" neighborhood, but with a certain low-key charm.

A handful of small, newly-landscaped city parks and playgrounds offer gathering places and green escapes for parents and kids. The 6 local train stops at 28th and 33rd Streets along Park Avenue and a number of city buses serve the area's avenues and streets.

Midtown

Financial institutions, law firms, high-end fashion, and luxurious hotels define Midtown Manhattan, located between the West Side Highway and Third Avenue and roughly between 40th and 60th Streets. Since Midtown is primarily a business district, during regular working hours it is one of the busiest parts of the City. Among the many attractions here are the famous Rockefeller Center, Saint Patrick's Cathedral and the fabulous, renovated Grand Central Terminal.

Midtown is a very desirable residential area as well. On the eastern side of Midtown there are a number of magnificent luxury towers offering breathtaking park views, the most impressive of these is Trump Tower. Located directly on Fifth Avenue, this building is the office and home of real estate magnate Donald Trump, who himself resides in its top floors.

The residential stars of Midtown's western front are Hell's Kitchen and Clinton. What was once a run-down district has become a vibrant, lively residential community. Both neighborhoods are home to an eclectic mix of young professionals and longtime residents. Ninth Avenue is lined with a new crop of chic bars, restaurants, shops and galleries.

Area residents love the convenience of walking to work, as well as some of the city's best-known restaurants—including The Russian Tea Room and Trattoria—exclusive shopping on Fifth Avenue, and the major bonus of having several different subway lines and Grand Central Terminal nearby. Many residents are public figures, celebrities, and other wealthy individuals, and some of the rents and sales prices here are among the City's steepest.

With all that Midtown has to offer, it is also the City's most tourist-filled zone. Seemingly the entire world celebrates New Year's Eve watching a globe drop from a flagpole atop the former Times Tower in Times Square. Though a few spins around Rockefeller Center's skating rink might be enough to get you to forgive the crowds and understand the sense of awe that this part of the city inspires.

Murray Hill

The Murray Hill section of Manhattan's East Side is located between Fifth Avenue and the FDR Drive and 34th and 40th Streets. It is considered by some to be the most ideal residential area nearest to the Midtown business district. The neighborhood combines elegant townhouses on side streets, attractive apartment buildings, plenty of restaurants and cafes and excellent transportation right in the middle—literally—of Manhattan. Neighborhood residents are a mix, including longtime residents who love the area's convenience and recent college grads.

Homes in Murray Hill represent a wide range of choices, from condos to co-ops and to brownstone apartments. One neighborhood highlight among an impressive collection of schools, libraries and cultural centers is the Morgan Library on the northeast corner of 36th Street and Madison Avenue, and the northeast corner at 37th Street and Madison Avenue is home to one of the City's most romantic mansions, the Beaux Arts building. Both lend elegance and style to the neighborhood. The venerable department store, Lord & Taylor, continues to have one of the City's most popular Christmas season window displays drawing crowds during the holidays. Other nearby landmarks are also the most useful: Grand Central Terminal and the MetLife building on Park Avenue and the New York Public Library on Fifth Avenue.

Sutton Area

Two of the city's most sought-after residential addresses, Sutton Place and Beekman Place comprise the neighboring enclaves of elegant—though not overwhelmingly so—buildings along the East River, east of First Avenue with Midtown to the west. With dramatic views of the Queensboro Bridge and Roosevelt Island and easy access to the F.D.R. Drive, these neighborhoods are tiny oases of calm and community amid hectic Midtown commerce.

Sutton Place benefits from two public parks. One Sutton Place South—a neo-Georgian style mansion—is one of the city's grandest addresses. Two townhouse rows—between 57th and 58th Streets—share a large communal garden overlooking the East River.

Beekman Place runs from 49th to 51st Streets, consisting of two blocks of ivy-covered townhomes and co-op buildings. The neighborhood was named for the Beekman family, which built its mansion, Mount Pleasant, there in 1764. The grand apartment house at One Beekman Place was built in 1929, setting the tone for the little street. One Beekman Place opens directly to the river, and its south facade overlooks the United Nations and its gardens.

Though the area is a bit far from the nearest subway on Lexington and Third Avenues, an upside is that housing prices tend to be below those of the Upper East Side. The neighborhood boasts plenty of retail activity, including the vast Bridgemarket Food Emporium just below the Queensboro Bridge. Sutton East Tennis Club, an enclosed winter tennis facility, is another convenient amenity for neighborhood residents.

Turtle Bay

When you step onto the grounds of the United Nations, you've not only left Manhattan, but you've exited the United States as well. The UN is considered to be International Territory owned by all of its member nations.

Fortunately, surrounding neighborhoods don't require a visa. Comprised of Sutton and Beekman Place and Turtle Bay, the area is a diplomatic playground and business center as well an enclave of East Side elegance. A highlight of Turtle Bay—between 41st and 53rd Streets, and eastward from Lexington Avenue to the East River—is the UN Plaza and park. Entry is free, and it boasts a beautifully-tended rose garden. An East River stroll is also an easy addition to life here.

Two of the City's most sought-after residential addresses, Sutton Place and Beekman Place comprise the neighboring enclaves of elegant buildings along the East River offering two public parks and a quiet residential setting. With dramatic views of the Queensboro Bridge and Roosevelt Island and easy access to the F.D.R. Drive, these neighborhoods are tiny oases of calm and community amid hectic Midtown commerce.

Though the area is a bit far from the nearest subway on Lexington and Third Avenues, the neighborhood boasts plenty of retail activity, including the vast Bridgemarket Food Emporium just below the Queensboro Bridge. Sutton East Tennis Club, an enclosed winter tennis facility, is another convenient amenity for neighborhood residents.

We've Reached The End

I hope you've gotten information from this book which will assist you in your search for a New York City zipcode. For any additional questions please e-mail me:

heidiberger@mac.com

Made in the USA
Lexington, KY
16 November 2014